Contents

Chapter 1

What Is the Internet?

The Internet is a tangle of wires and cables, a huge **network** that ties millions of computers together from all over the world. As long as computers are connected to the Internet, they have the ability to talk to each other.

The Internet's Roots

In the early 1960s a group of scientists at the U.S. Department of Defense faced a challenge. Their jobs required them to constantly share information with other scientists, researchers, and military officials. Often the information was needed very quickly. The answer, they were convinced, was computers—but the computers were sometimes thousands of miles apart.

In 1962 the Advanced Research Projects Agency (ARPA) was formed to solve this problem. A man named Joseph C.R. Licklider was hired to lead computer research. Earlier that year he had written several memos about a "Galactic Network" that he envisioned in the future. He called it a "thinking center," a huge computer network that would span the entire earth. It would be extremely powerful and accessible by computers everywhere.

Other scientists agreed that Licklider's dream was possible. In 1965 researchers from ARPA and the Massachusetts Institute of Technology (MIT) developed a plan for the network. Then they designed

A woman carefully works on a computer that was built in the 1960s.

and built it. Computers from different locations would be able to contact each other through a telephone line connection. Information could then be shared between the computers. This would only be possible if the information, called data, was formed into small packages of information known as **packets**. Once the packets arrived at their destination, they would be reassembled into their original form.

After three years of development, the network—called **ARPANET**—was ready to test at two major universities. The computers it would be tested on were nothing like today's small, portable laptops and desktop models. Each of these computers was bigger than a refrigerator.

A Successful Network Test

In October 1969 computers at the University of California at Los Angeles and the Stanford Research Institute in Menlo Park, California, were connected. Students at each of the schools tried sending messages to each other. When one of the students typed the "G" in "LOGIN," the system crashed, but the second attempt worked fine. The test was declared a success. A few months later computers from universities in Santa Barbara, California, and Utah were added to the network. ARPANET consisted of four computers. Because they shared information with other computers, they were known as **hosts**.

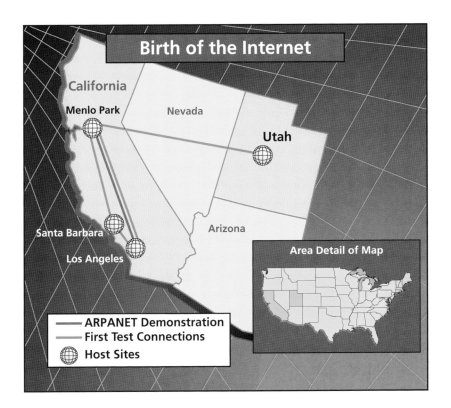

Birth of the Internet

California
Menlo Park
Nevada
Utah
Santa Barbara
Los Angeles
Arizona

Area Detail of Map

— ARPANET Demonstration
— First Test Connections
⊕ Host Sites

For the next two years scientists continued to modify ARPANET to make it work better. They also added more hosts to the network. This caused problems because the computers were not exactly alike and did not always work with each other. So scientists developed **protocols**, or special instructions that all computers could understand.

The Network Grows

Finally the network was ready to show the outside world. In October 1972 an international computer conference was held in Washington, D.C. Scientists demonstrated ARPANET by linking computers together from all over the United States. Computer scientists from Great Britain, France, Italy, and America attended the conference. They were impressed with the demonstration. They were also excited about what the new network would be able to do.

In 1974 computer scientists Vinton Cerf and Bob Kahn developed a new protocol for ARPANET. It was designed to make the network perform better as more computers were connected. Cerf wrote a paper about the new protocol, and he referred to the network as the "Internet."

During the 1970s more computers hooked into the network. An article in the *Magazine of Fantasy and Science Fiction* describes how fast it began to grow:

> It was difficult to stop people from barging in and linking up somewhere-or-other. In point of fact, nobody "wanted" to stop them from joining this branching complex of networks, which came to be known as the "Internet". . . . The more the merrier. Like the phone network, the computer network became steadily more valuable as it embraced larger and larger territories of people and resources . . . ARPANET . . . was a curiosity for a while. Then computer-networking became an utter necessity.[1]

New Features, New Functions

Throughout the 1970s and 1980s more hosts were added. What started as a network with just four computers had become much more. Now it was a network of networks.

As ARPANET continued to grow, new features were added that made it useful for more people. Electronic mail (**e-mail**) made it possible to send messages from one computer to another. Mailing lists allowed users to send the exact same e-mail to large numbers of people. On-line **newsgroups** began to appear and they soon became very

Vinton Cerf (left) and Robert Kahn (second from right) pose with other computer scientists at a science-awards ceremony in Spain in 2002.

popular, as one writer describes: "The discussion groups, or 'newsgroups,' are a world of their own. This world of news, debate and argument . . . is rather like an enormous billowing crowd of gossipy, news-hungry people, wandering in and through the Internet on their way to various private back-yard barbecues."[2]

Lightning-Fast Growth

By 1984 more than a thousand hosts were on the network and it was growing faster than anyone expected. To identify each of the hosts, and keep

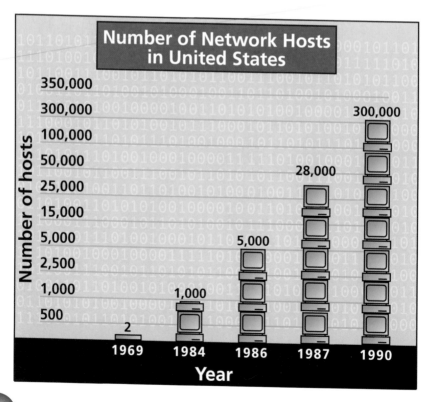

Number of Network Hosts in United States

The Internet

them separate from each other, **domain name servers** were introduced. These were suffixes such as .com (pronounced "dot-com") for commercial establishments, .edu for educational institutions, .org for nonprofit organizations, and .gov for government organizations. These suffixes, along with many others, are still in use today.

More than five thousand hosts existed by 1986, and the network was still growing. In 1987 there were twenty-eight thousand hosts, and three hundred thousand by 1990. Finally the original ARPANET was discontinued. What had started as a communications device for a government organization was now something totally different. From that point on the huge network of networks would only be known as the Internet.

Chapter 2

The Internet Goes Mainstream

The Internet continued to grow more popular, but it was mysterious and hard to understand. Only people with technical knowledge were able to figure out how to use it. For one thing, searching for host computers was impossible. Even after they were found, keeping track of their location was impossible. People had to build their own lists of sites if they wanted to return to them. Of the thousands of computers on the Internet, each had its own password. So if someone's list had hundreds of sites, there were also hundreds of different passwords.

Once a connection was made with another computer, information could be accessed—but that was difficult too. Users had to stumble their way through a complicated maze of terms such as FTP programs, index files, archives, and subcategories. Plus they had to type commands in precisely the right order. If even one symbol was typed incorrectly, the host computer would not understand and it would not respond. It was a tedious, time-consuming process to gather information from the Internet. So most people did not bother with it.

Simplifying the Internet

Alan Emtage was not one of the people who had trouble understanding the Internet. As a computer science graduate student in Montreal, Canada, he

A computer scientist at CERN updates pages on the World Wide Web.

had a great deal of technical knowledge. He did, however, believe that searching for information should be easier. So he wrote a program that "crawled" through the Internet and searched for things based on key words. Once it found information that matched the words, it created an index. The program was called **Archie**, which was the word "archive" without the "v." When other students and professors heard about Archie, they were eager to use it too. In 1990 Emtage released it for public use. It later became known as the world's first **search engine**.

Linking Information

Another computer whiz who wanted to simplify the Internet was Tim Berners-Lee. He was a software consultant for an organization in Switzerland called CERN. Berners-Lee was very familiar with the Internet and the information that was available. Like Emtage, though, he believed finding and retrieving information was difficult for most people. For years he had wondered how the problem might be solved. He shares what often went through his mind: *"Suppose all the information stored on computers everywhere were linked,* I thought. *Suppose I could program my computer to create a space in which anything could be linked to anything.* All the bits of information in every computer at CERN, and on the planet, would be available to me and to anyone else. There would be a single, global information space."[3]

Pictured is the computer that ran the first World Wide Web server in 1990.

In 1980 Berners-Lee wrote the program in his spare time. At first he created it just for his own personal use and named it "Enquire." He explains what the name meant: "[It was] short for *Enquire Within upon Everything,* a musty old book of Victorian advice I noticed as a child in my parents' house outside London. With its title suggestive of magic, the book served as a [doorway] to a world of information, everything from how to remove clothing stains to tips on investing money."[4] He believed that his program would act in a similar way—opening up the world of information that was on the Internet.

It was ten years before Berners-Lee started creating a new version of Enquire. He had become convinced that CERN had a great need for it. Also, he believed that researchers, scientists, educators, students, and just about anyone else could benefit from it. He decided to name it **WorldWideWeb**. Later he would change the name. He did not want people to confuse the program with the information space that he called the **World Wide Web**.

Spinning the Web

Developing the web software involved many different steps. One was to create a method of addressing pages, to give websites their own locations on the Internet. Berners-Lee called this the universal resource locator (**URL**). Also, just as the Internet needed a protocol for computers to work together, the web would need one as well. So he developed the hypertext transfer protocol, more commonly known as **HTTP**. He then developed a programming system known as hypertext mark-up language, or **HTML**. This would help connect information together, and allow **links** to be hidden on web pages. The links would provide access to other places within a website, and also to other sites. The last step was to create a **browser**. This would allow users to see the program on their computer screens.

Berners-Lee finished the web program in the summer of 1991. He explains how it was designed to work: "The Web is an abstract (imaginary) space of information. On the Net, you find computers—on the Web, you find document[s], sounds, videos . . . information. On the Net, the connections are cables between computers; on the Web, connections are hypertext links. . . . The Web could not be without the Net. The Web made the Net useful because people are really interested in information (not to mention knowledge and wisdom!) and don't really want to know about computers and cables."[5]

Tim Berners-Lee makes a point as he speaks at an Internet conference in 2001.

In the fall of 1991 Berners-Lee announced his new program on several Internet mailing lists. He made the browser available to people for free. He did not want to charge for it because he believed it would be more successful if no one owned or controlled it.

Amazing Growth

At first not many people were aware of the program. By 1993, two years after Berners-Lee made it available, there were 130 sites on the web. Then word began to spread, and the World Wide Web started to grow—fast.

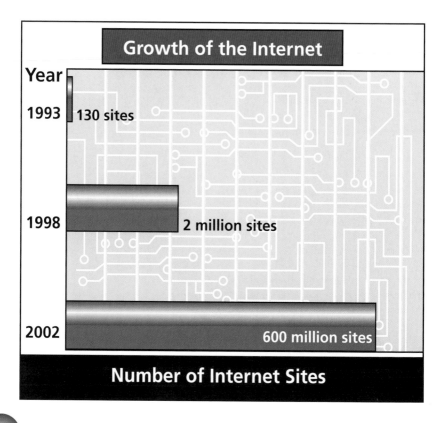

Growth of the Internet

Year	Number of Internet Sites
1993	130 sites
1998	2 million sites
2002	600 million sites

A family explores the Internet with great interest.

By January 1996 there were one hundred thousand sites. Two years later that number had jumped to more than 2 million. According to a survey by an Internet research group, in September 2002 there were more than 600 million sites worldwide.

A U.S. government report entitled "The Emerging Digital Economy" says that use of the Internet has grown faster than any other technology in history. Radio existed for nearly forty years before its audience reached 50 million. Television was around for thirteen years before that many people tuned in. Then the web was created and suddenly the Internet was open to everyone in the world. Its audience grew past 50 million too—but unlike radio and television, it happened in just four years. The World Wide Web made that possible.

Chapter 3

How People Use the Internet

Mary Raines cannot imagine life without the Internet. Originally from New Zealand, she now lives in Japan where she teaches English as a Foreign Language (EFL). She often visits websites that have been created by other EFL teachers. Like Raines many of them are teaching in countries that do not have reference materials available. So they use the Internet to share their ideas with teachers from all over the world. Raines finds a variety of teaching ideas and lesson plans on the web. Plus, she finds solutions to problems that she faces in her job, as she explains: "Sometimes students ask me questions I can't answer—about, say, the cultures and customs of English-speaking countries other than New Zealand. I can find out about these things quickly on the web. I don't have access to good English libraries here, so the web is my library for this sort of thing."[6]

The World's Biggest Library

Like Raines, people everywhere use the Internet as a reference source. Thousands of periodicals, such as newspapers, magazines, and journals, are available on-line. Many public libraries have their entire collection of periodicals on the Internet. Also, public library sites allow people to search for books by subject, author, or title.

Old or hard-to-find resources also can be found on the Internet. One example is a website called The Internet Library of Early Journals. This is a digital library that includes the complete text of journals published in England during the 1700s and 1800s. One such journal is "The Annual Register, or a View of the History, Politicks, and Literature of the Year 1758."

A deaf woman uses the Internet to wish holiday greetings to a friend.

Another journal on the site is "The Gentleman's Magazine: Or, Trader's Monthly Intelligencer."

ThinkQuest is an on-line library that was created especially for young people. One section is the ThinkQuest Challenge Library. It contains links to more than five thousand websites. The sites cover most every topic—from art history to martial arts, from homework help to artificial intelligence. All the sites have won awards and all of them were designed by kids.

No matter what sort of information people seek on the web, they need to know where to start. So that is where search engines can help. There are thousands of them, and some of the most popular include Google, Dogpile, Yahoo, and About.com. They perform a similar function to Archie, the original search engine. These, however, are much faster and more sophisticated. Users enter key words and the search engines look for sites that include those words.

On-Line Entertainment

Just as people use the Internet to find information and do research, they also use it for fun. For example, people who love art may dream of visiting the Louvre, a famous art museum in Paris, France. Traveling to France may not be possible, though, so they can visit the Louvre on-line. The museum has nearly four hundred thousand works of art in its collection. Every piece is colorfully displayed on the Louvre's website.

A web page (left) provides a guide to the Louvre museum where two couples (above) admire a large painting.

A woman explores the Internet while walking on a treadmill at a gym.

On-line games are another popular use of the Internet. People can play everything from checkers to chess, as well as card games such as solitaire on websites. A site called Pogo.com includes word games, trivia games, sports games, and puzzles. Funbrain.com uses games to help kids learn math, science, and history. It also helps young children learn how to count and spell, and uses hidden clue games to help with reading skills.

Parents often use the Internet to help entertain and teach young children. Becky Vollink, the mother of a four-year-old girl named Emma, often visits the Nickelodeon site. She finds recipes that she and Emma can make together, and ideas for crafts. Also, the site has a coloring book. Emma uses the computer mouse to "paint" her favorite *Dora the Explorer* and

Blues Clues cartoon characters. She also learns songs that are played on the website, and she sings along with them.

Buying Anything—from Anywhere

Some people like to shop as much as they like to play. On the Internet they can buy most everything they need without ever leaving their homes. There are on-line cooking stores, furniture stores, clothing

Use of the Internet can help busy people simplify their lives.

stores, and toy stores. On-line flower shops offer an assortment of bouquets, plants, and gifts. On-line travel services let people search for the best vacation deals. The U.S. Postal Service site sells postage stamps for mailing and collecting.

Randi Trygstad depends on the Internet for her shopping. She owns an advertising agency, and is also the mother of nine-month-old twins. Her life is busy and she has very little free time. She explains how important the Internet is for her: "I did every bit of my Christmas shopping on the Web this year, and I also used it to buy other gifts, like for birthdays and weddings. When I need anything for Jake and Riley [her twins], I can find whatever I need—even if I can't find it anyplace else. It is an amazing time saver for me and frankly, using the Internet helps me keep my sanity!"[7]

Selling On-Line

Trygstad also spends time on eBay, the on-line auction site. When she did her spring cleaning, she found things that she no longer needed. So she took digital photos of the items and listed them for sale on eBay. She sold everything and made about a thousand dollars.

On-line booksellers are some of the most popular sites on the web. Barnesandnoble.com and amazon.com sell millions of titles each year. Also, for customers who do not need brand new books, the sites feature links to used booksellers. Mary Raines tells why she likes these sites: "In Japan, foreign books

How the Internet Works

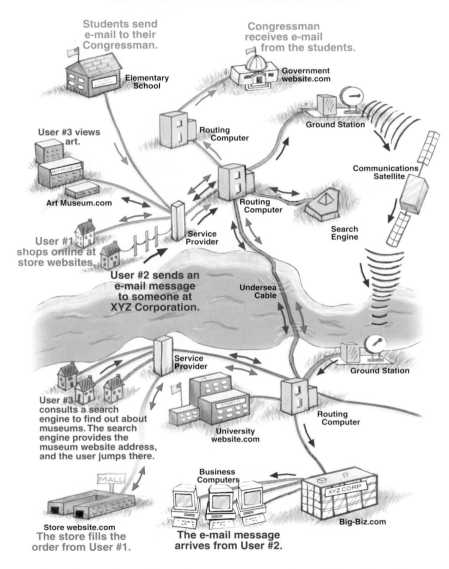

Students send e-mail to their Congressman.

Congressman receives e-mail from the students.

Elementary School

Government website.com

Ground Station

User #3 views art.

Routing Computer

Communications Satellite

Art Museum.com

Routing Computer

Search Engine

User #1 shops online at store websites.

Service Provider

User #2 sends an e-mail message to someone at XYZ Corporation.

Undersea Cable

Service Provider

Ground Station

User #3 consults a search engine to find out about museums. The search engine provides the museum website address, and the user jumps there.

University website.com

Routing Computer

MALL

Business Computers

XYZ CORP

Store website.com
The store fills the order from User #1.

The e-mail message arrives from User #2.

Big-Biz.com

This chart shows how the Internet works. Follow the color-coded arrows and text to see how people communicate, shop, and view images from their computers through the Internet.

How People Use the Internet **27**

[those written in English] are expensive, plus the choices are very limited. I can find whatever I need on Amazon. The only problem is, I find SO much that I could go broke if I visit too often!"[8]

A New Way of Talking

Because Raines lives in Japan, she is far away from her home in New Zealand. She counts on e-mail to keep in touch with family and friends all over the world. She writes to people at home, as well as those from Australia, Greece, Malaysia, Thailand, and England. She also e-mails friends in Sweden, the United States, Turkey, France, Guam, and Hong Kong.

Another way people use the Internet to communicate is through instant messaging or on-line chats. These features allow users to have instant conversations on their computer screens. There are many such programs, including America Online Instant Messenger, Yahoo! Messenger, and ICQ.

There are hundreds of different ways that people use the Internet. Whether they shop or chat with friends, play games or research ancient history, they can find most anything they want on-line. Trygstad sums up her feelings about it: "Ten years ago, if someone would have told me I would be so dependent on a computer, I would have said they were nuts. But when I look at my life, and how much I use the Internet, I don't know how I could survive without it. I suppose I could . . . somehow. But I just can't believe how much easier life is because of it."[9]

Chapter 4

The Internet's Effect on Society

There is no doubt that the Internet has made life easier for people. It has also affected society in a number of other ways. Many people believe that the changes have been a good thing. Others do not agree, and they blame the Internet for negative changes. Some people are even afraid of it.

Net Crime

One of the reasons people fear the Internet is crime. Since the Internet has grown so popular, on-line crime has soared. Criminals find ways to break into other people's computer systems to steal bank account numbers and other personal information. They can also break into business or government websites to cause damage. This is called **cracking**, and the people who do this illegal activity are called **crackers**.

One of the most serious problems is crime against children. In 1998 a sheriff in Virginia made a disturbing discovery. He found that 20 percent of missing teenagers had disappeared because of someone they met on the Internet. This is a problem in other states too. A national survey was done in 2000 involving children ages ten to seventeen. About one-third said that someone on the Internet had asked to meet them. Many said they received suspicious telephone calls or obscene photos, and some were physically threatened. This is known as **cyberstalking**. According to J.A. Hitchcock, an

A detective instructs children in an Internet safety program. Some stalkers contact their victims on the Internet.

author and well-known expert on Internet crime and security, forty-five states now have cyberstalking laws. She explains why:

> When the first cyberstalking cases were reported, no one knew what to call it. We're not talking about two people arguing or calling each other bad names. These were incidents where it went beyond being annoying and had become frightening. Yet states didn't have laws in place to protect victims, and their harassers kept up the harassment—which escalated sometimes to real-life stalking situations.[10]

Criminals have also been caught cheating people in on-line auctions. In 1999 a New Jersey woman was arrested for offering Beanie Babies and Furbies for sale on eBay. People paid her for the items, but she never sent their purchases. The same type of situation happened in North Carolina. A seller used different screen names and offered toys, jewelry, and collectible items on an on-line auction. When people received their items, they found that he had lied about their value and condition. In some cases they never received the items at all.

Law enforcement agencies are aware that there are many different types of Internet crime. They also know that it is a serious issue. The Federal Bureau of Investigation (FBI) and state and local police departments are working together to protect people and catch those who are guilty.

Adam Yauch (MCA) of The Beastie Boys performs onstage. The Beastie Boys allow fans to download their music from the Internet for free.

Can Music Really Be Free?

Some people believe that another type of Internet activity is a crime: downloading music. The first website that allowed this was Napster, created by Shawn Fanning. The site made music available in a digital format known as **MP3**. People could visit the site and get whatever music they wanted for free. Some musical artists, such as the band Metallica, fought this because they considered it stealing. The recording industry was also against it. Other artists, such as the Beastie Boys and Limp Bizkit, did not agree. They encouraged the practice because they believed it would help sell their music. Eventually Napster was sued for **copyright** violations. This meant that Fanning did not have permission to copy and distribute music that was owned by other people.

Fanning was found guilty and Napster was shut down. However, other websites have taken its place. Some sites are legal because the artists have given permission for their music to be used. There are also restrictions, such as not being able to copy music onto a CD. The Recording Industry Association of America, however, has vowed to stop all music swapping. The association has filed lawsuits against offenders. Still, the sites are very popular with music fans. Because of the Internet they now have access to a wider variety of music than ever before.

Controversies

People disagree about whether the Internet has helped or hurt the music industry. Many feel the same way about communication. Stanford University did a study on how the Internet is changing people's lives. It found that about 25 percent of those surveyed spent less time with friends and family because of the Internet. The people admitted that they often used e-mail instead of talking with others on the phone or in person. The professor in charge of the study says the Internet does help people communicate with their friends and family more often, but he explains why this is not always a good thing: "E-mail is a way to stay in touch, but you can't share a coffee or a beer with somebody on e-mail or give them a hug."[11]

Not everyone believes the Internet has hurt communication. Randi Trygstad is someone who believes that the opposite is true. She lives in Michigan and her parents live in Boston. She has a sister in Boston, one in England, and one in Washington, D.C. She has family members in other states too. She explains why e-mail is valuable to her: "My twins change so much every day. My

A girl laughs at the video her mother has made. Sending clips of digital video by e-mail to friends and family has become very popular.

family can't be here to see them when they are being funny or goofy, or when they're looking so innocent in their sleep. So I take digital photos, and e-mail them to my mom and dad, my sisters, and other family members. That makes them feel like they're sharing the moments with me."[12] Trygstad says that e-mail has not taken the place of real conversations with her family. She talks to them often on the telephone and sees them as much as ever. She just believes the Internet makes it easier for her family to be closer.

Education

Just as the Internet has changed communication, it has changed the way people learn. Students may connect to classrooms from home. They can even get a variety of college degrees on-line. In many schools students have advantages they never had before. One example is the North Slope Borough School District in northern Alaska. It is an isolated, remote area that covers thousands of miles. There are eight villages in the district and the schools are hundreds of miles apart. Some of the villages can be reached only by airplane or snowmobile. Now elementary and high school students use **videoconferencing** in their classrooms. This allows them to see and hear each other on computer monitors as they talk. Videoconferencing helps the students feel more closely connected to the world outside their villages.

A young boy learns to use the Internet at a boys and girls club.

Students at a Canadian high school had a different kind of learning experience because of the Internet. They heard about two explorers who planned to ski to the North Pole, which was more than twelve hundred miles away. The students thought it would be interesting to keep track of the men. So they set up an e-mail connection with them. The men had portable computers and were able to connect to the Internet via German satellite. As they moved toward their destination, they answered the students' questions. The students built a special website and recorded the information on it. This project, called "Follow Us," helped the students learn about Arctic exploration at the exact time it was happening. When the project was over, the students felt almost as if they had made the journey with the explorers.

The Internet and Literacy

Studying on the Internet has helped adult learners too. A group of adult literacy students in Albany, Oregon, participated in an "electronic field trip" to the South Pole. They learned about native wildlife such as penguins and fish, and plants that survive in very cold areas. Also, they talked to scientists about their education and training. The students found the project exciting, and it motivated them to learn. Plus it helped them improve their reading and writing skills.

There are many other examples of how the Internet has helped improve literacy. One involved third graders at an elementary school in Baltimore, Maryland. These were low-income students, and many were too poor to have telephones in their homes. Most of them had reading skills that were below their age levels. In a special experiment the school installed computers and Internet connections in their homes. The students used the computers for a year and then their reading skills were tested again. More than 80 percent had improved their reading levels by at least one grade. Studies have also proven that the Internet helps students improve other skills, such as writing, math, and critical thinking.

Only Time Will Tell

The Internet has changed society in many ways. Some effects have been positive and others have been negative. There are people who believe the Internet has made life much better, while others wish it did not exist at all. No one knows for sure how big the Internet will grow. Nor do they know exactly what it will look like tomorrow or how it will affect society. What is known, though, is that the Internet will continue to change. As it does, society will adapt and change along with it. History has already proven that.

Chapter 1: What Is the Internet?

1. Bruce Sterling, "Short History of the Internet," *Magazine of Fantasy and Science Fiction*, February 1993. www.forthnet.gr/forthnet/isoc/short.history.of.internet.
2. Sterling, "Short History of the Internet."

Chapter 2: The Internet Goes Mainstream

3. Tim Berners-Lee, *Weaving the Web: The Original Design and Ultimate Destiny of the World Wide Web by Its Inventor.* New York: HarperCollins, 1999, p. 4.
4. Berners-Lee, *Weaving the Web*, p. 1.
5. Tim Berners-Lee, *Frequently Asked Questions.* www.w3.org/People/Berners-Lee/FAQ.html#What2.

Chapter 3: How People Use the Internet

6. Mary Raines, interview with author, April 11, 2003.
7. Randi Trygstad, interview with author, April 4, 2003.

8. Raines, interview with author.

9. Trygstad, interview with author.

Chapter 4: The Internet's Effect on Society

10. J.A. Hitchcock, interview with author, April 20, 2003.

11. Quoted in Kathleen O'Toole, "Study Offers Early Look at How Internet Is Changing Daily Life," *Stanford News*, February 16, 2000. www.stanford.edu/dept/news/pr/00/000216internet.html.

12. Trygstad, interview with author.

Glossary

Archie: The world's first search engine, developed by Alan Emtage of Montreal (the word "archive" without the "v").

ARPANET: The first network, which eventually developed into the Internet. It was a project of the U. S. Department of Defense's Advance Research Projects Agency.

browser: A feature of a web program that allows a user to see information on a computer screen.

copyright: The legal protection against copying or distributing work, such as music or art, without permission.

cracker: Someone who "cracks" into a computer.

cracking: The act of illegally breaking into a computer by bypassing its security system.

cyberstalking: The act of following someone into chat rooms or other on-line forums to threaten or harass them.

domain name server: Suffixes such as .com, .org, .edu, and .gov that identify hosts and keep them separate from each other.

e-mail: Electronic mail—a way of sending messages over the Internet.

host: A computer connected to the Internet.

HTML: Hypertext mark-up language—a programming language used for most websites.

HTTP: Hypertext transfer protocol—the special protocol, or instructions, used for the web.

link: A way to move from one page to another within a website, or from one site to another.

MP3: Music that has been converted to a digital format to maintain quality while reducing the size.

network: Two or more computers that are connected so they can communicate and share information.

newsgroup: An on-line discussion group for sharing information, usually on a specific topic.

packet: A unit of information that can travel across the Internet.

protocol: A special set of instructions for the Internet and the web.

search engine: A searching mechanism that crawls through the web to find information.

URL: Universal resource locator—the string of symbols that is used to identify anything on the web.

videoconferencing: A meeting or conversation between people in separate locations, made possible by video equipment and the Internet.

World Wide Web: The information space on the Internet that is accessible because of web software.

WorldWideWeb: The name that Tim Berners-Lee first gave to his web program.

Books

David Jefferis, *Cyber Space: Virtual Reality and the World Wide Web.* New York: Crabtree, 1999. Covers a wide variety of topics, including the positive and negative aspects of the Internet.

Charnan Kazunas and Thomas Kazunas, *The Internet for Kids.* New York: Childrens Press, 2000. An interesting and simple introduction to the Internet.

Josepha Sherman, *History of the Internet.* New York: Franklin Watts, 2003. A story about the people involved in creating the Internet, and how the network grew into what it is today.

Periodicals

Monkeyshines, "The Information Age: Computers and the Internet," July 2001. An informative article about the history of the Internet and the web.

Mary Vincent, "Living in a Wired World," *Owl*, September 2002. Discusses how schools around the world use the Internet.

Internet Sources

Alexander Colhoun, "But—I Found It on the Internet!" *Christian Science Monitor*, April 25, 2000. www.csmonitor.com. An article about how more and more students depend on the Internet for research.

Websites

How Stuff Works (www.howstuffworks.com). Includes information about the Internet, including e-mail, search engines, Internet radio broadcasting, and the future of the net.

Learn the Net (www.learnthenet.com). An informative and interesting site that covers Internet basics, web surfing, newsgroups, and many other topics.

Yahooligans! (www.yahooligans.com). Designed especially for kids, this site is an excellent guide to the many features of the web. Includes games, music, jokes, and answers to all types of questions.

Index

Picture Credits

Cover Photo: © Mason/Science Photo Library
© Bettman/CORBIS, 5
Suzanne Santillan, 7, 10, 18, 27
© Reuters New Media Inc./CORBIS, 9
© David Parker/Photo Researchers, Inc., 13
© CERN/Science Photo Library, 15
© AFP/CORBIS, 17
PhotoDisc, 19, 25
AP/Wide World Photos, 21, 30, 36
COREL Corporation, 23
© Neema Frederic/CORBIS SYGMA, 24
Reuters/Landov, 32
© George Shelley/CORBIS, 34

Peggy J. Parks holds a bachelor of science degree from Aquinas College in Grand Rapids, Michigan, where she graduated magna cum laude. She is a freelance author who has written a number of books for various Gale Group divisions, including KidHaven Press, Blackbirch Press, and Lucent Books. Parks lives in Muskegon, Michigan, a town that she says inspires her writing because of its location on the shores of Lake Michigan.